FENG SHUI

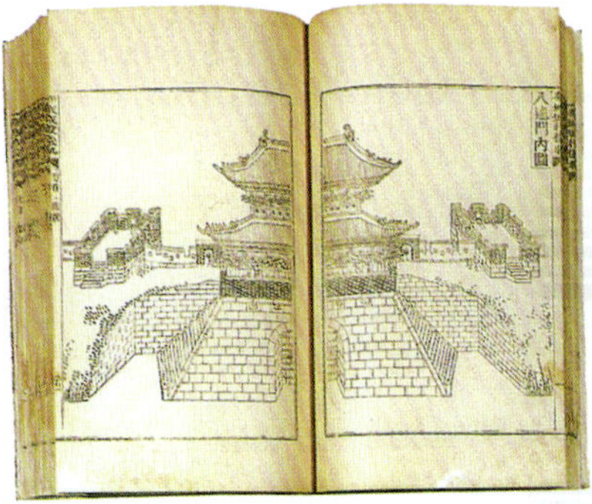

ANCIENT WISDOM FOR THE NEW AGE

FENG SHUI

THE SECRETS OF HARMONY

Sonya Hwang

IMM lifestyle books

Read. Learn. Do What You Love.

Text, illustrations, and photographs by IMM Lifestyle Books, an imprint of Fox Chapel Publishing, 903 Square Street, Mount Joy, PA 17552. *www.foxchapelpublishing.com*

First published in 1998 by New Holland (Publishers) Ltd

Designed and edited by
Complete Editions
40 Castelnau
London SW13 9RU

Editorial Direction: Yvonne McFarlane
Editor: Michèle Brown
Designer: Peter Ward

ISBN 978-1-5048-0158-4

Printed in China
First Printing

70%
FSC
www.fsc.org
MIX
Paper | Supporting responsible forestry
FSC® C147414

To learn more about the other great books from Fox Chapel Publishing, or to find a retail near you, call toll-free at 800-457-9112 or visit us at *www.FoxChapelPublishing.com.*

We are always looking for talented authors. To submit an idea, please send a brief inquiry acquisitions@foxchapelpublishing.com.

Or write to:
Fox Chapel Publishing
903 Square Street
Mount Joy, PA 17552

This is a gift book. It is not intended to encourage diagnosis and treatment of illnesses, disease or other general problems by the layman. Any application of the recommendation set out in the following pages is at the reader's discretion and sole risk.

CONTENTS

Across the Millenia 7 Yin and Yang 12
Check Your Balance 14 The Five Forces 16
Five-Element Relationships 24
Flowing Ch'i 28 The Eight Trigrams 32
Astrology and Feng Shui 36
Protective Animals 38 Dragon Lines 40
Animal Formations 44
Five-Force Mountains 46
Direct Directions 48 The Nine Palaces 50
Mirror, Mirror 54 Floral Feng Shui 56
Neighbourliness 58 Harmony at Work 61

ACKNOWLEDGMENTS 64

ACROSS THE MILLENIA

Though feng shui is fashionable today to ease the cares of life, it emerged from the hardships of the agrarian Chinese over 3,000 years ago. Meaning "wind and water", it developed from the early shamanistic teachings going back to the Emperor Fu Hsi, who originated the first *I Ching,* or *Book of Changes.* He formulated the original Eight Trigrams, groups of three lines representing yin and yang forces, from patterns he saw on a tortoise's shell.

Another legend tells of a cripple who was bequeathed the fabled *Book of Power Over the Waters,* which enabled him to stem the flooding River Lo. Through this wisdom he rose to be the Emperor Yu, devoting his efforts to codifying the essential forces of the earth. His system, the Later Heaven Pa-k'ua (the octagonal, or circular, symbol made up of the eight Trigrams) existed side by side with Fu Hsi's Earlier Heaven Pa-k'ua. Fu Hsi's system indicated the ideal situation of the day, while Yu's predicted change. Feng shui developed as an offshoot of *I Ching,* through the bad Shang Dynasty, into the Chou Dynasty founded by King Wen, who refined the *I Ching* system as a means of prediction. His son, the Duke of Chou, added his book of commentaries to form the three volumes of *I Ching* we know today.

Earlier Heaven

Later Heaven

Another legendary figure was the fabled Yellow Emperor Huang-ti, who lived around 2700 BC. He allegedly lost his way when he was fighting a bandit chief, who had invoked magical powers to cloak the mountains with fog. The Lady of the Nine Heavens appeared to his aid and gave him the knowledge and use of the compass, which remains a feature of feng shui today. This was passed to King Wen's grandson, who used his compass and knowledge of the Earlier Heaven pa-k'ua to find favourable locations for his palaces. These early emperors added the study of the heavens to their great knowledge of all that was on earth. Primitive calendars were devised and during the Shang period and in the following Chou Dynasty the Celestial Stems were matched to the Five Elements. By the time of Confucious the twelve animal symbols had come into use.

Out of the mists of fable, feng shui slowly emerged as a favoured way of divination, but it was not until the Tang Dynasty of the 9th century AD that a recognisible text devoted to it was produced. It was inspired by the spectacular mountains of the Kuei-lin province. Here the scholar Yang Yun-sung started the "form" school of feng shui, identifying the mountains with animal shapes, principally the Dragon and Tiger. Soon after other schools sprang up, notably a consolidation of the Compass or Eight Directions Method, the Eight House Method and the Flying Star School.

The Form and Compass Schools are interlinked and both absorb many of the mythical traditions, which do not appeal to purists. Titles of learned works have been passed down, but what writings there are appear to be the work of later and lesser writers.

During the Sung Dynasty, from 960 to 1279 AD, more feng shui scholars appeared and a school, the Thirty-Six Meridians, was founded. It produced a treatise on mountain forms and shapes, providing propitious backgrounds for residential or burial sites.

The study of buildings in relation to their environment is known as yang or positive feng shui. But there is another aspect, that of yin or negative feng shui. This relates to the oldest use of the art, applying not to the houses of the living, but those of the dead. The shaman or feng shui practitioner would be consulted about the funeral rights, the alignment of the grave and the date of burial. So surrounded by magical myths were these ceremonies that when a relative died in a far distant place, if the practitioner could divine a propitious resting place in his home town, he could summon the physical body from one tomb to another.

And so, from across the millenia, we can summon the wisdom of Fu Hsi and his Trigrams, King Wen and his *I Ching,* which together have gone into the formulation of feng shui, to help us cope with the stresses and strains of every day life.

YIN AND YANG

These are the basic energies of the universe, in a constant state of flux according to the months and years, the seasonal changes, the time, the astrological conditions and the internal flow of body energies.

Yin is the essential female element in the eternal scheme of things. It is the mystery of the depths of the night, the sleeping earth in winter, the Moon, the female cycle and creativity. Yang is the vital male element. It is the light of the Sun, strong and firm, confident and certain, the cycle of the seasons.

In feng shui, yin refers to the serene, inactive parts of a room, unimpeded by doorways, windows or other apertures. Yang represents the vital area where action takes place, doors, windows or other openings. The aim of the feng shui practitioner is to arrange the room in such a way as to balance the yin and yang forces. The strength of these forces is measured with the use of the Lo'Pan compass, which is described later.

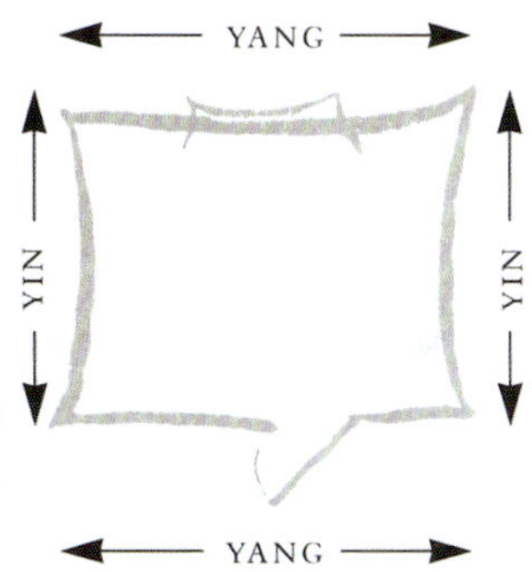

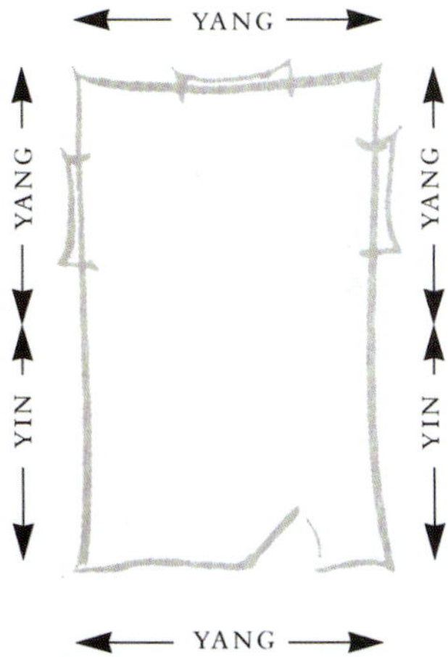

CHECK YOUR BALANCE

Yin places: woodland, meadows, shady bowers, quiet mountainsides suggestive of meditation, calm seasides.

Yang places: cities, sunny locations, flat landscapes for an active life, office blocks, rugged mountains for climbing.

Yin buildings: long and narrow, elegant skyscrapers.

Yang buildings: set square on the ground, squat, square.

Yin outlook: the shaded side of the house or office.

Yang outlook: the sunny side of the house or office.

Yin type: tall, slim, generous features, supple frame.

Yang type: short, broad, tight features, sturdy frame.

Yin mind: creative, imaginative, intuitive.

Yang mind: logical, quick-thinking, ordered.

Yin emotions: gentle, sensitive, insecure, depressive.

Yang emotions: strong, ambitious, confident, irritatable.

Yin colours: green, blue, pastel shades.

Yang colours: yellow, orange, red, bright shades.

Yin forms: rounded, long, slim, elegant.

Yang forms: square, angular, compact.

Yin materials: natural fabrics, natural woods.

Yang materials: manufactured metals, glass, polished stone.

As we have seen, yin and yang are in a constant state of flux. Remembering this, you can see how the various attributes above, when inverted, make a scale from gentle to strong, from tall to short. You can consider your own personality by taking this scale into account and adjust your lifestyle accordingly.

THE FIVE FORCES

Water

The first of the basic forces of feng shui is Water, expressed as a wavy, irregular line. It suggests hidden depths as well as shallows. Its surface may be calm, but there are eddies below, suggesting turbulence and change. Its colour is black and it represents winter, when the hard ground must be prepared for planting.

When the seeds are planted, mysterious growth takes place hidden below the surface. Its material is glass, the ice it can form on its surface.

Water governs speech and communication. It represents deep feeling and hidden power.

Metal

The second basic force is Metal, expressed as the sinking sunset, particularly autumnal. It is related to swords or ploughshares and its colours are white or metallic gold and silver. Its symbol is a disc or other circular shapes, possibly related to coins.

The materials mostly associated with metal range from modern stainless steel to ancient bronze, also favouring copper, brass, gold and silver. It is also the sign of marble and harder stones such as granite. Its qualities reflect those of solidity and reliability, ploughing and delivering the crops, as well as those of leadership and inspiration, marching ahead, sword in hand. But this is not done recklessly. Metal's energy is carefully harnessed and can strengthen the weaker tendencies of the other forces.

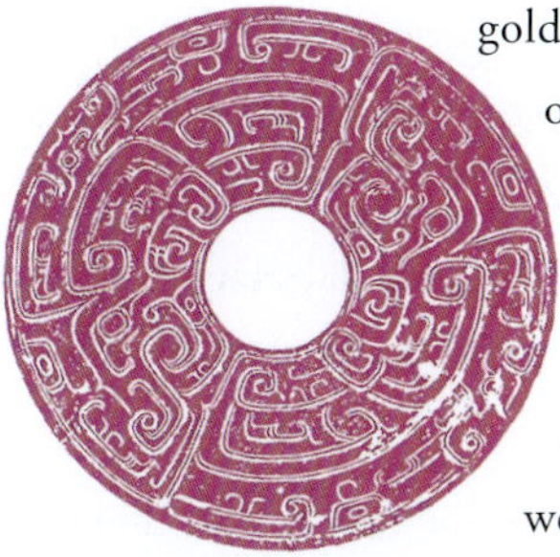

Earth

The third of the basic forces, the centre one, has no direction or season, although some feng shui practitioners have allocated it to the south-west and north-east. Its symbol is any flat shape and it represents earthy colours, such as ochre and burnt umber. These reflect the colours of the earth in central China. It shapes are usually low and squat, be they for buildings or pieces of furniture.

It represents all natural materials, for building or decoration. Bricks and softer stones, such as limestone, natural fibres, such as cotton and silk, as well as clay and ceramics.

It is the force of caution and steadfastness. In the home it is a force for stability and warm surroundings.

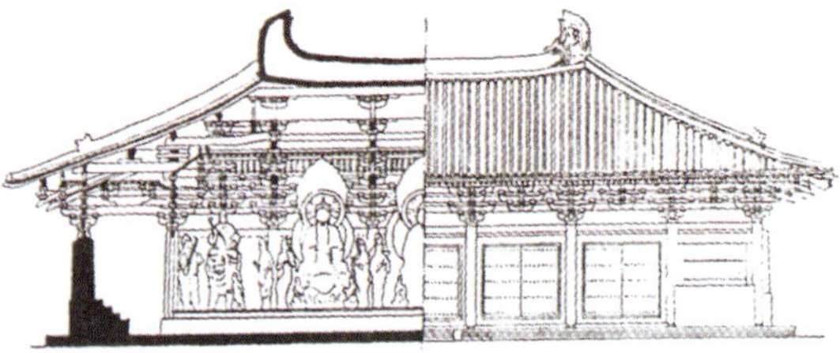

Fire

The fourth of the basic forces is expressed as the heat of the sun, summer and the south. It produces animal life and its colour is red. Its symbol is triangular, echoing the shape of flames, and its attributes are reflected in buildings and mountains.

With the right compatriots, such as tall trees associated with Wood, people living in Fire buildings are thought to produce exceptionally bright children.

Fire's materials are few, as it can have a deleterious effect on them. Modern plastics, with their invariably bright colour are associated with the force, but are recommended with due consideration as they are also associated with negative energies.

Fire represents passion and commitment, vital energy which can invigorate an environment, having an equally invigorating effect on those who live and work there. This passion is tempered by a generous warmth.

Wood

The last of the basic signs encompasses all growing vegetable life and is related to spring, the new sunrise and towards the

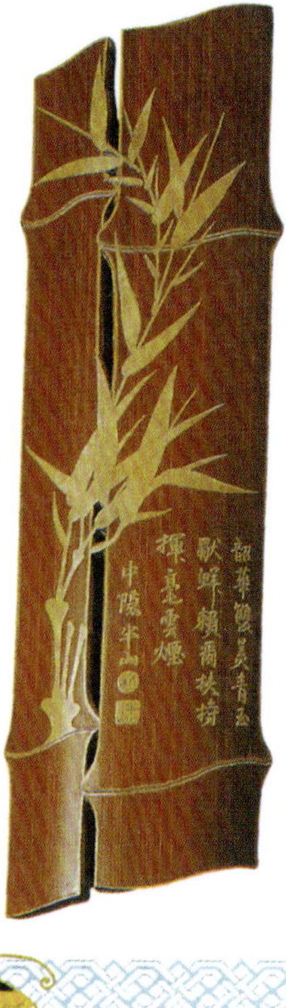

east. Its colour is plant green, often with a tinge of blue to reflect the sky, or the China Sea. Its symbol is any tall shape, a tree trunk or a skyscraper.

Its materials are all natural products, derived from vegetation. In the Orient houses may be built out of them. In the West it is more likely that natural wood, wicker, bamboo and paper will be found in the furniture and decorations of a home or office.

Its qualities are those of life, associated with growing and sexual activity.

FIVE-ELEMENT RELATIONSHIPS

The Five Elements affect each other in a variety of ways. Each strengthens the next in the sequence and weakens the next but one of the sequence. The positive sequence is: WOOD burns, producing FIRE which creates ash EARTH from which is produced METAL which melts like WATER which feeds WOOD.

The negative sequence is: WOOD takes away nourishment from EARTH which pollutes WATER which puts out FIRE which melts METAL which cuts WOOD.

When confronted with a problem of conflicting forces these sequences can inform.

Fire is best countered by a strong force such as Water. If the Fire force is dominant, Water elements can be introduced into the premises, paintings of water, blue-green objects and water itself. Fire can also be countered by making it nourish Earth and expend energy weakening Metal, so a ceramic pot in a metal stand might be the thing.

Earth is weakened by Wood, drained when feeding Metal and dissolved when absorbing Water. These powers can be combined by introducing a glass vase or container with growing plants. Metal alone can also be employed in

the form of moving metal objects, perhaps an oriental mobile or chimes.

Wood is cut down by Metal and drained when it feeds Fire. Metal objects are most efficacious, in the form of sculptures, clocks or other ornaments. Similarly, Fire can work in the form of red furnishings or paintings. Strong lights also conjure Fire, but may not be aesthetically acceptable. A typical oriental combined light and fan works well.

Metal is weakened by fire and drained when nourishing water. It is best countered by its opposite, Fire, as represented by red objects or furnishings. Water can also help dissipate Metal, so paintings of watery scenes might help. Both can be combined if red-coloured water, or another liquid, is displayed in an elegant glass container.

Water is weakened by Earth, drained by Wood and dissolved when putting out Fire. To counter negative energies, earthen ceramics may be employed. It can also be neutralised by displaying wood carvings or other objects.

FLOWING CH'I

This is the flow of energy which links, in a web-like fashion, man to the land and so to the entire cosmos. It can be likened to ley lines, connected to western sites such as Stonehenge and Carnac.

The power lines in the Orient appear in healing systems such as Shiatsu and acupuncture, as well as being the basis of feng shui. It is the incarnation of yin and yang and is in a constant state of flux. The ch'i energy which we take in from our surroundings influences all our moods and actions. It flows through solid matter, which is why it can influence the "mood" of buildings. Negative ch'i can linger in the dark, dank parts of old building, concentrating the doleful yin energy. It enters freely through doors and windows, which is why their placement is important, and can also slowly permeate walls.

In general ch'i is a positive force as long as the flow is

unimpeded. It should be allowed to meander and flow, without coming up against brick walls. It can be deflected by mirrors, explained later, and should not be allowed to rush straight through a house, for example, along a corridor joining front and back doors, or, similarly, through windows situated opposite each other. It will not only be unable to pass on its invigorating energy, but may take some out with it. A path which winds its way to an entrance encourages positive ch'i and deflects negative sha.

Other unfavourable and negative ch'i energies can be engendered by unsuitable building materials, particularly synthetics. Air conditioning systems can cause havoc by forcing the ch'i energy off its natural course. Dark corners and gloomy corridors slow down the flow, creating an air of lethargy which can be passed on to the inhabitants with deleterious effects.

Bad angles confuse ch'i in its flowing path. A sharp cornered piece of furniture at a bad angle to another is unsettling.

There is an actively bad life force which is quite the opposite of ch'i, known as sha. Unlike swirling ch'i, sha energies shoot out in straight lines, like an arrow. It is thought that the slow development of the railway in China was due to the fear of straight, sha lines.

Sha can also be invoked by the presence of outhouses, other properties, roads or powerlines aimed at the building at sharp angles and straight lines. Diversionery action must be taken, by planting trees, erecting mirrors or even moving small buildings.

Sha should not be encouraged by straight drives or pathways directly to a building's entrance. Zig-zag or winding paths are preferred. If a straight drive has been inherited and vehicle access is not needed, tubbed plants or rock formations should be employed, perhaps in association with bushy plant borders.

THE EIGHT TRIGRAMS

The Eight Trigrams feature in many types of divination and mystical systems, having been first devised by the Emperor Fu Hsi some 2000 years BC. Each one is made up of three yin or yang lines in different combinations. These in turn combine to make 64 Hexagrams. They each represent a different type of energy and are each assigned qualities of the Five Elements, previously explained. Each one is also assigned a direction, which is important in divining the direction of forces within a room or house.

☰ **Ch'ien.** Direction Northwest, element Metal, all yang, can be the beginning or the end, for it is collective wisdom at the end of a cycle and the wisdom to start anew. It is a male sign, connected with the father, but today can relate to the principal wage-earner. At work it is the manager, the organiser. Its colour is silvery-white, age, winter and wisdom.

☵ **K'an.** Direction North, element Water, yang enclosed by yin, thus softening it. Conception and then the wheel of fortune, which is life. At work, wheels feature: garages, machinery, travel. It relates to calm, spirituality and sexuality. Its off-white colouration suggests translucence and change. It is a sign of mid-winter and the deep thoughts of the night.

☶ **Ken.** Direction Northeast and element Earth. The younger son learns by leaving the home in search of knowledge. Its symbol is a mountain, which must be climbed metaphorically. It is brilliant white, reflecting the loving nature of parents for whom he could be a late blessing.

☳ **Chen.** Direction East and element Wood, with thunder as its symbol. This is the eldest son, with the responsibilities of inheritance. The yang lower line (the first) moves easily up through the two yin lines to blosssom like a sunrise. This is get-up-and-go, carry on the family line, and unbridled energy, naturally coloured green.

☴ **Sun.** Direction Southeast, with the element Wood. This is the eldest daughter, expected to take on responsibilities of the home before achieving her own. This is continuity, the gentle yin line heavily protected by the two yang lines above. But being the first gives her strength of her own. With the symbol of Wind, she will find her own direction.

☲ **Li.** Direction South, with a Fire element. This is the middle daughter who might work unrecognised until the older marries. Hard work will pay off and recognition, a husband or successful career will result. This is the Cinderella sign, put-upon, but remaining cheerful until the prince comes along. Her symbol is fire.

☷ **K'un.** Direction Southwest and element Earth. This is the mother of the family, offering nourishment and succour to those surrounding her. The direction can be disruptive, but these are the forces mothers must contend with. Though the three yin lines suggest multiplied gentleness, they give each other the strength to look after children, run hospitals and maintain family harmony. Unexpectedly her colour is black.

☱ **Tui.** Direction West and element Metal. The upper yin line is seriously supported by the two lower yang lines, which means let go and relax, you have built up sufficient mental and physical reserves to do so. Its symbol is the lake, a calm surface with strong support below, often financial. Related to the youngest daughter, an element of fun and joy is added, shown by its colour, red.

ASTROLOGY AND FENG SHUI

In Chinese feng shui, the Big Dipper (or Plough) constellation points to the North Star during all four seasons. Its nine stars (seven visible and two "companions") correspond to nine positive or negative orientations which form the basis of feng shui and its Japanese version, Nine Ki. Ki is the equivalent of the basic life force, Ch'i. Central

to both versions is the use of the Luo Shu or Magic Square, discovered during the development of the philosophical treatise *I Ching*.

In China, practitioners of Nine Ki astrology use their charts of the cycles of the earth's energy (a sequence of nine years) to determine a person's Ki (or Ch'i) energy in their birth year, as well as month and day. From your Nine Ki number is found the basis for assessing your character, most advantageous time to maximize your energy level and the best time to make changes in your macro or micro environment.

PROTECTIVE ANIMALS

Just as they feature in Chinese astrology, so in feng shui animals give protection in the form of particular land formations. They are derived from animal spirits recorded by ancient shamans or priests. They are full of beneficial energy and are effective blocks to destructive energy.

The Green Dragon is high land, hill or mountain on either side of a site. They guard from the left, the strength of protection depending on their particular form.

Similarly, the White Tiger protects the right. The Red Raven protects from in front and can be a modest outcrop which does not

block the view. The Black Tortoise guards the back and should not dominate the site. Facing the site,

the Green Dragon is to the left and the White Tiger to the right.

HIGH
WHITE
TIGER
SITE
SITE
WHITE
TIGER

DRAGON LINES

When looking at a site, or a possible home, to assess its feng shui potential, the surrounding terrain is of supreme importance. The most prominent feature to take into account is the Dragon, or mountain or hill. This is analysed, with its various peaks or outcrops identified.

They are the Dragon's head body and limbs. Any streams or rivers which cross the terrain are known as the Dragon's veins. They are said to emanate the breath of the Dragon, the paths of the earth's energy. Dragon veins also have magnetic fields which assist the feng shui interpreter.

In ancient times, communities which lived under the benign spirit of the Dragon would prosper. It is thought that without the Nine Dragons (Kowloon in Chinese) to the north of Hong Kong, its outstanding prosperity would not have been achieved.

Dragon veins can be classified as kingly, ordinary,

coherent or scattered. The kingly veins appear in mountain ranges with peaks, ridges and valleys. Ordinary veins are in smaller ranges. Coherent veins should form a continuous

path around the chosen site, the "arms" of the mountains or hills enfolding it. Scattered veins are difficult to decipher as there may well be small coherent groups within an apparently random pattern of veins.

The beginnings and ends of the veins are classified to determine the strength of their influence. A gradual decline, with the hills merging gradually with the plain, suggests the energy of the Dragon being absorbed back into the earth. Abrupt ends of the ridges means that the Dragon energy has not been given the chance to wind down, such signs not portending well for towns or cities located at such points.

On plains or seemingly featureless terrain good fortune can still be traced. Though the Dragon brings the best fortune, the patterns of rivers, lakes and even man-made waterways can also be a good omen.

In towns and cities, the outline of the rooftops can be treated as Dragons, with the traffic flow emulating rivers and streams.

ANIMAL FORMATIONS

Some particularly auspicious landscape formations appear to have animal shapes. A whole manual can be compiled of these particularly powerful formations. They are thought to have absorbed the power of both the sun and the moon, the basic yang and yin forces. Energy stored in basic animal forms, such as Tiger in Waiting, Phoenix Stretching, Crane Standing, is limited and will not regenerate when absorbed by a house or burial site, and so only one generation or the first owner will benefit.

Dynamic animal formations, suggesting an animal in motion, such as Flying Dragon, Snake in Panic, Lion with Ball or Tiger Roaming, are active. They can store and gather energy, as well as spread it. Several generations will benefit.

FIVE–FORCE MOUNTAINS

In feng shui, mountains are classified according to their shape and are categorised as the Five Elements (i.e. Water, Earth, etc.). A similar principle therefore applies to buildings.

Water Mountains. Uneven mis-shapen mountains, often with round tops. Buildings which fall into this category have irregular shapes, odd spires, a mixture of roof types, curved features and varied additions over the years.

Metal Mountains. These have gentle slopes and rounded peaks. Metal buildings have rounded or domed roofs and arched doors and windows.

Earth Mountains. These have steep sides and flattened tops. Buildings are low and flat-roofed, most often domestic accommodation.

Fire Mountains. These are triangular and have steep

peaks. Buildings are those with pointed roofs such as churches or buildings of pyramidal shape.

Wood Mountains. These are similar to Earth Mountains, but the gentle slopes lead to a slightly more rounded top. Tower blocks or churches without spires come into this category.

Most land- or city-scapes have a mixture of these shapes. In feng shui there are 24 combinations which are regarded as powerful places with concentrated energy pathways. An example would be when a Water Mountain meets a Wood Mountain, nourishing it, as we have seen by the inter-element relationships. Wood merges smoothly into the ground, offering firm foundations. This would be a site of wealth and prosperity.

DIRECT DIRECTIONS

The tool of the feng shui practitioner is the Lo'Pan or compass, so-called because it traces the energy flow on a web-like arrangement of divisions resembling a network, Lo'Pan being the Chinese for net plate. The basic compass has nine rings and is placed on a straight side of the object aligned with the direction from which the reading is made.

The centre of the compass is known as Heaven's Pool or Tai Chi, which marks the starting point of life's breath. The first ring, going outwards, is marked with the Eight Trigrams, described in the following pages. This gives the relative strength of yin and yang and the passage of the seasons from winter yin to summer yang. The second ring has the Nine Stars, the Dipper and two companions. They reflect the shape of nine mountains. The third ring follows the position of a further 24 mountains, which correspond to directional points on a mariner's compass. The fourth ring lists the eight Tzu Wei stars from the Tzu Wei, Pole Star, system of astrology. The fifth and sixth rings are inscribed with the 64 Hexagrams, the total possible combinations of the Eight Trigrams. Those in the fifth ring refer to the present, those in the sixth tell of the future. The seventh ring has the 24 terms of the solar calendar still in use today. The eighth ring contains the 28 constellations and is used to determine the time and position for burial. The ninth, outer, ring is divided into 360 degrees.

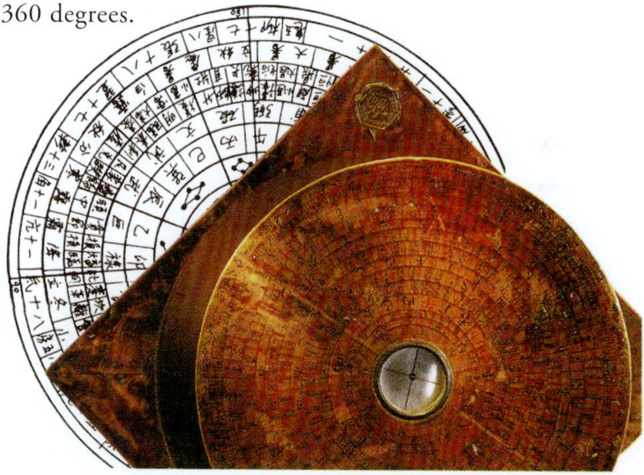

THE NINE PALACES

These are the eight directions of the compass, plus the centre, which reveal the flow of good and bad forces. The eight positions each have a related Trigram and are identified by a number/colour pairing called a star. The basic arrangement of the palaces is the Magic Square, in which the numbers, arranged in three rows, add up to 15 in all directions.

Direction	*Trigram / Palace*	*Number/ Colour (Star)*	*Element*
north	k'an (water)	one-white	water
south-west	k'un (earth)	two-black	earth
east	chen (thunder)	three-jade	wood
south-east	sun (wind)	four-green	wood
centre	none	five-yellow	earth
north-west	ch'ien (heaven)	six-white	metal
west	tui (lake)	seven-red	metal
north-east	ken (mountain)	eight-white	earth
south	li (fire)	nine-purple	fire

The Magic Square was devised by Emperor Fu Hsi, who formulated *I Ching.* It is both a map and a timetable for the feng shui practitioner. It helps with problems such as when to move house or make a journey. Five is always at the centre and it can be rotated either clockwise or anti-clockwise.

4	9	2
3	5	7
8	1	6

clockwise

6	1	8
7	5	3
2	9	4

anticlockwise

MIRROR, MIRROR

Mirrors are powerful tools in feng shui as they both deflect and reflect, which equates with warding off evil and magnifying good. They encourage the flow of positive Ch'i and dissipate harmful Sha. The ancient Chinese venerated mirrors as doors into the beyond. They used the Trigrams, the same as those of *I Ching,* to make symbols to place on the back of mirrors.

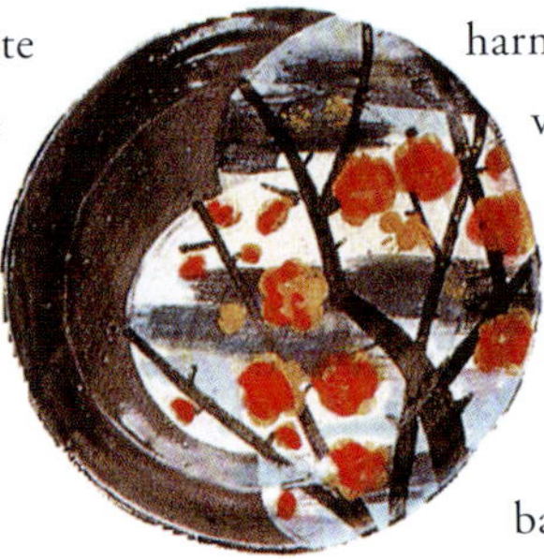

In practical feng shui, mirrors can be used to reflect light into a dark, yin, area which attracts lethargy. They can be placed on north walls to bring in some extra sunny yang energy when needed. A tall mirror in a hallway can be used to counter the "knife-edge" image of an inward opening door. If the main doorway is exactly opposite that of a neighbour, a mirror suitably placed can deflect potential conflict. A similar precaution can be taken if there is a tree or lamp-post directly outside. Convex mirrors can deflect excessive energies, such as might occur when your main entrance is directly opposite a road junction. The placing of mirrors in the bedroom is crucial, if you have to have them at all. The ancient Chinese believed that if the dreamer's soul caught sight of itself it would take fright and leave the body. If a mirror is necessary or part of a dressing table, it should be positioned so that the head of the bed is not reflected.

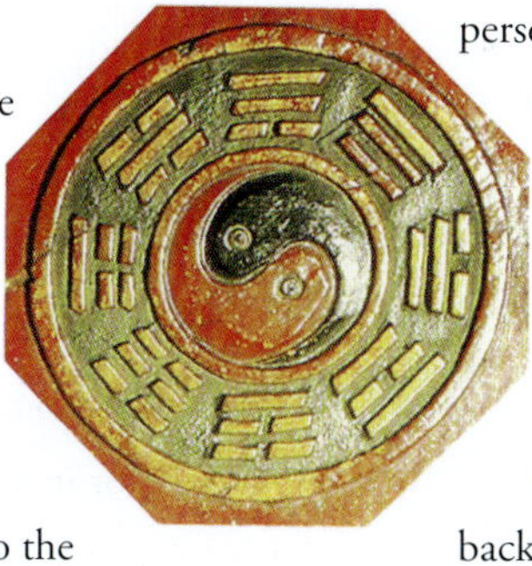

Although personal design preferences have to be taken into account, in difficult situations the most powerful mirror is in the form of an octagon, with the Eight Trigrams displayed or at least attached to the back.

FLORAL FENG SHUI

Flowers can play an important part in enhancing chi energy depending on their colour and shape.

Cornflower: Its clear blue opens up lines of communication and its star shape helps outgoing personalities. Delphiniums have a similar effect, their tall stems having Wood energy.

Carnation: Reds and pinks are very romantic, whereas white is for dignity.

Lily: A calming influence in over-energised areas, through their combination of tall stems and downward pointing flowers.

Sunflower: The power of the sunflower with its Fire energy has only recently become accepted. Combined with their Earth energy, this makes for a stabilising influence.

Rose: Traditionally related to romance, red roses and their Metal energy really do increase chi energy, especially when placed in the west.

Iris: These quietly introduce some stronger chi energy through their Wood energy, especially the purple variety.

Tulip: Metal energy is contained in the bowl-like flowers. Red can induce romance, pink, sensual pleasure when placed in the west. White brings repose, when placed in the north-east.

NEIGHBOURLINESS

Neighbourly friction can be aggravated, explained and avoided by the comparative shape of each house.

Water buildings can lead to sluggish feelings when they are surrounded by Wood buildings. Some extra Water features will give added energy. When near Fire buildings, there can be disharmony. Some Wood energy, such as plants, is needed. When close to Earth buildings, there can be a threatening atmosphere. Some bright Metal relieves the tension. The perfect, uplifting, atmosphere is created when the Water building is surrounded by Metal.

Metal buildings near Water are financially unfavourable. Build up Earth and Metal, shrubs or bright metal work. Encircled by Wood buildings suggests you may be having a restraining effect on your neighbours. Additional Water energy will help. When ringed by Fire you will have financial problems as Fire burns Metal. Earth energy is needed. When Metal buildings are surrounded by Earth features, property financial returns can be expected.

Earth buildings enclosed by Metal buildings lead to insecurity, which can be alleviated by some Earth and Fire features. Water added to Earth dilutes it with loss of vitality. Metal is needed, perhaps some bright metal garden furniture. Wood in proximity leads to insecurity, which can affect health. Literally, Fire is needed. Earth buildings surrounded by Fire features have a warm family atmosphere.

Fire buildings dominated by Earth buildings suggest that the occupants will be held back. Wood energy is needed, perhaps in the form of tall trees. Metal buildings in proximity affect the whole area detrimentally. Your contribution could be added Earth features, possibly in the garden. Water buildings flood Fire buildings, putting the occupants under some type of threat. Reach for the sky with Wood energy, perhaps more tall trees. Fire buildings blend profitably with Wood buildings, making you a key figure in your community.

Wood buildings are singed by Fire properties surrounding them, leading to the threat of a career going up in smoke. Add a Water feature, such as a garden pond. When circled by Earth buildings there can be aggravation in the area. Clear the air with Fire energy, such as inventive lighting. Metal encircles Wood, limiting energy and vision. Water is needed. Wood buildings are enhanced by the presence of neighbouring Water buildings, giving clarity of vision and purpose.

HARMONY AT WORK

Harmony at work is deeply influenced by the Nine Palaces and their related Number/Colour stars. The principles laid down centuries ago for the location of a Chinese home can bring good fortune to a business, whilst engendering favourable relations amongst the employees. That it may be an ultra-modern office block or shop will make it no different from a traditional Chinese building.

Buildings faced with bright red bricks belong to the Fire element and will attract associated problems. Those covered with reflective surfaces are sending away much energy, as do large glass panels.

The placing of the entrance is important. If it is determined that there are combinations of six-white and eight-white, one-white and six-white or six-white and eight-white stars, these are auspicious signs, as they are the stars of wealth, prosperity and fortune. Avoid two-black and three-jade stars, or take remedies to change them, as they presage enmities in the work-force. A fountain near the entrance is most fortunate, particularly when set in a large reception area which acts as a gatherer of energy.

It is preferable for lift doors to be shielded from the reception area as they sweep the chi energy too quickly through the building. Large mirrors should be avoided, as they deplete energy. However, they can be used if the placement of the door in relation to the approach road encourages bad, sha forces.

If you are able to choose your position within the office area, do not choose a space facing a lift, as this will create much negative energy. Be as far away from the parking area as possible, particularly if the building is built over one. Vehicular movement has a destabilizing effect.

The location of your desk is also important, and the associated star influence. Do not place it under an exposed beam which will "crush" potential success. The best position is six-white and eight-white as this predicts success in business. It is best to face a window or a square with a neutral combination. Those to avoid include two-black and three-jade or seven-red and six-white, as they predict rivalry and underhand methods.

Plants enhance a working environment, those directly related to the Five Elements having particular force. The Hyacinth, related to Wood, is an upright plant with uplifting ch'i energy. The Palm, related to Fire, brings vibrant yang energy with it, making it ideal for "dead" corners. The Cyclamen or Begonia, related to Earth, encourage office romance without causing upsets. The Peace Lily, related to Metal, has in recent years been found to have a calming effect in computer environments, thriving on electrical radiation.

ACKNOWLEDGEMENTS

The illustrations are from the National Museum of Korea, the National Palace Museum, Taipei, Libraire Viollet, Paris, Fotogram, Spain, the Corcoran Collection and Grapharchive, London.

The publishers have made every effort to identify all illustration sources. Any errors and omissions will be corrected in future editions.